A Concise History And Description Of Kenilworth Castle

Kenilworth castle

Nabu Public Domain Reprints:

You are holding a reproduction of an original work published before 1923 that is in the public domain in the United States of America, and possibly other countries. You may freely copy and distribute this work as no entity (individual or corporate) has a copyright on the body of the work. This book may contain prior copyright references, and library stamps (as most of these works were scanned from library copies). These have been scanned and retained as part of the historical artifact.

This book may have occasional imperfections such as missing or blurred pages, poor pictures, errant marks, etc. that were either part of the original artifact, or were introduced by the scanning process. We believe this work is culturally important, and despite the imperfections, have elected to bring it back into print as part of our continuing commitment to the preservation of printed works worldwide. We appreciate your understanding of the imperfections in the preservation process, and hope you enjoy this valuable book.

A CONCISE HISTORY

OF

Kenilworth Castle, &c.

KENILWORTH CASTLE has been long celebrated in the annals of this Kingdom. In the times of our warlike Barons, it was renowned for superior strength; and in latter days, when security rendered its use, as a fortress, unnecessary, after being enlarged and greatly ornamented by the Earl of Leicester, it became the scene of one of the most sumptuous entertainments that was ever offered by a subject to his Sovereign. The beauty and grandeur of the remaining ruins, correspond with the magnificent ideas one has been led to form of this Castle, and bear indisputable testimony of its ancient splendour. It was built about the year 1120, by Geoffry de Clinton, a Norman, who was Lord Chamberlain and Treasurer to King Henry the First, of whom he obtained a grant of land for this purpose.

THERE was formerly a more ancient Castle in this parish, situated in the woods opposite Stoneleigh Abbey; but it was demolished in King Edmund's wars with the Danes, long before the foundations of the present Castle were laid.

THE Monastery for Black Canons, near the church (the gateway and part of the chapel of which are still remaining), was founded by the same Geoffry de Clinton, who endowed it with large estates, and various privileges; particularly, a tenth part of all the eatables that were brought into the Castle, though they had been tithed elsewhere before, together with all the lamb skins throughout his manors, and a right to fish in the pool, with boats and nets, every Thursday.

THIS Priory suffered much during the siege of the Castle, in Henry the Third's Reign: for though they allowed the King three hundred quarters of corn, and sundry other things, to obtain his protection for the rest of their goods, yet they were pillaged by the soldiers, and so far impoverished, that the King granted them letters patent after the Castle surrendered, recommending to all his tenants to contribute to their relief, as far as they were able.

At the Survey, taken in the twenty-sixth year of Henry the Eighth, this monastery was valued at £643. 14s. 9d. and on the 15th of April, in the twenty-ninth year of the same reign, (about four hundred and thirty years after its first endowment,) was surrendered by Simon Jekys, the last abbot, and sixteen monks, who had pensions assigned them by the King. His Majesty granted the abbey-lands to Sir Andrew Flamock, whose grand-daughter and sole heiress carried them by marriage to John Golbourn, Esq. who afterwards buying some horses, that had been stolen out of Lord Leicester's stables, was so much frightened by the threats of the Earl, that he was glad to make his peace, by giving up the lands to him on easy terms; and they have been ever since annexed to the domains of the Castle.

The Castle, though it seems to have been in possession of the son and grandson of the founder, did not continue uninterruptedly in the

Clinton family. In the eleventh of Henry the Second, the Sheriff accounted to the Crown for the profits of the park; and in the nineteenth year of the same reign, (A. D. 1173,) it was garrisoned by the King, on his son's rebellion; at which time it appears, by an account of the stores laid into the Castle, for the use of the garrison, that wheat was about twopence halfpenny per bushel, barley near the same price, the carcase of a cow salted, was charged at two shillings, cheese fourpence apiece, and other articles in proportion.

In the beginning of King John's reign, Henry de Clinton, grandson to the founder, released to the King all his rights to the Castle, with the woods, pools, &c. and it was afterwards never out of the possession of the Crown, till granted by Henry the Third to the Earl of Leicester, as appears from the charges of the different Sheriffs and Governors, for repairs; in which, from time to time, considerable sums of money were expended. It is also evident, from the Sheriff's account of the farm of the lands, for feed of hogs in the park, ward-money paid by the country people, in lieu of personal service in guarding the Castle, and rent paid by divers persons residing therein, who are supposed to have obtained permission to live there, from its being a place of security for themselves and goods, in those turbulent and licentious times.

Henry the Third, in 1242, new built the outer wall on the south side towards the pool; he likewise ornamented the chapel, and made a royal seat in it for himself and his Queen; but he did not long continue to make this the place of his residence, for about two years afterwards, he granted it to Simon Montford, Earl of Leicester, (to whom he had given his sister in marriage) for his own and his wife's life.

The woods about it at this time were so thick, that they became a shelter to thieves and outlaws, to the great annoyance of travellers; for whose safety six acres in breadth were ordered to be cut down on the road from Coventry to Warwick.

Montford, though he had received many marks of favor from Henry, was excited by his ambition, to form a scheme for subverting the government of the kingdom. The weakness, the injustice, and the partiality of this Prince for foreigners, whom he had raised to the most exalted dignities in the state, made the English Barons highly averse to his government. They sided with Leicester; and finding themselves too strong to fear any opposition, they carried their point, and instituted an executive council of twenty-four Peers, to assist in governing the kingdom: a most dangerous alteration of the constitution, but fortunately it was not of long continuance. The tyranny of their new rulers soon led the people to regret the change. Prince Edward, King Henry's eldest son, taking advantage of the general discontent that prevailed, and supported by some loyal Peers, and the King's military vassals, raised an army to deprive the Barons of their newly-acquired power. He was joined by the King, and they met the army of the Barons near Lewes, in Sussex; a general engagement ensued, in which the latter was victorious, and made the King, his brother, and the Prince of Wales prisoners. The Prince, however, making his escape, was soon enabled to raise another army, and attacking the Barons, who had made Montford their General, near Evesham, totally defeated him. He himself was slain, and the remains of his army, with his son, fled to Kenilworth, and shut themselves up in the Castle.

Prince Edward having thus released his father, whom Lord Leicester had kept in custody, marched with him and his victorious troops, to lay siege to the Castle. Young Montford going privately to France, in order to obtain assistance from his uncle, to support his friends, left Henry de Hastings, governor, during his absence, who gallantly defended the Castle for six months against the King's forces. But, at length, the garrison being in great want of provisions, attacked by a pestilential disease, and seeing no probability of young Montford's being able to bring them any assistance, were obliged to capitulate.

Stone balls, sixteen inches in diameter, and weighing near two hundred pounds, supposed to have been thrown with engines in this siege, are mentioned by Camden to have been dug up in his time; and some of them have been found within these few years.

The King's attention was not wholly taken up during the siege, with military affairs; he gave his niece in marriage here, to the Duke of Brunswick; and the Queen and her ladies came from Windsor, and honoured the camp with their company on that occasion.

A short time before the Castle surrendered, the celebrated decree called *Dictum de Kenilworth*, was made here, by twelve persons, Bishops and Peers, chosen by the King. This was done, in order to soften the severity of the Parliament holden at Winchester, which had entirely confiscated the estates of the rebels and their adherents, instead of which, this decree, that they might not be rendered desperate through despair, sentenced them only to a pecuniary fine, of not more than five years' income of their estates, nor less than two.

But to return to the Castle, which, by this means, coming again into the hands of the Crown, the King, in 1267, granted it, with free chase and free warren, and a right to hold a weekly market, and an annual fair, in Kenilworth, to Edmund, his younger son, whom he created Earl of Lancaster, two years afterwards.

The *pool* had, at this time, two mills standing upon it, and was about half a mile long, and a quarter of a mile broad.

In 1279, there was a great resort of noble persons to this Castle, consisting of an hundred knights and as many ladies, who formed a *round table* (a custom of great antiquity, to prevent disputes about precedency.) Many noblemen from foreign countries came here, on the occasion, and spent a week with the knights and ladies, in feasting, martial tournaments dancing, and other amusements. And so very distant from our ideas of luxury, were our forefathers, in those days, that an historian has thought it a thing worthy of recording, that the ladies who attended this festivity, were clothed in *silken mantles*. Roger Mortimer, Earl of March, was the principal promoter of this entertainment.

The Castle continued, uninterruptedly, in the possession of Edmund's successors, till the reign of Edward the Second; when another rebellion proved as fatal to the owner, as the former one had done to his predecessor, Lord Leicester.

The unbounded prodigality with which this

weak Prince lavished riches and honors upon his favourites, excited the murmurs of his subjects; and, in that warlike age, discontent was quickly followed by opposition; they flew to arms, and were headed by the Earl of Lancaster. Their resentment was first directed against Piers de Gaveston, the son of a Knight of Gascony, who was then the reigning favourite. Edward had granted to this young man the Earldom of Cornwall, and lately given him his niece in marriage. Intoxicated with the height of power to which he saw himself advanced, he treated the English Barons with haughtiness and contempt. They determined to be revenged, but on Gaveston's retiring to Flanders, were seemingly satisfied. The King, unable to live without his favourite, soon recalled him from thence. The Barons appeared in arms, and laying siege to Scarborough Castle, where Gaveston then was, forced it to surrender, carried him prisoner to Warwick Castle, and soon afterwards caused him to be beheaded on the top of Blacklow Hill, near Leek-Wootton. A cross was afterwards erected on the spot, in memory of Gaveston; and his name, cut in the rock below, is still visible. The King, whose fondness of favourites rendered him inattentive to the voice of his subjects, soon supplied Gaveston's place. Spencer, a comely young man, was the object he fixed upon. The same causes produced similar effects. The Barons formed a combination against young Spencer, and caused him and his father to be sentenced to perpetual exile. The King, unable at this time to resist so powerful a confederacy, was obliged to submit, but, sometime afterwards, taking the advantage of a small army he had raised to punish an affront offered to the Queen, he suddenly turned his arms against the Barons, who being quite unprepared to resist him, were obliged to fly. The Earl of Lancaster retreated towards the north, with what men he was able to get together, but being closely pursued by the King, and meeting another body of the royal forces in his way towards Scotland, he was repulsed in a skirmish with them, and taken prisoner.

As he had formerly shewn no mercy to Gaveston, he was treated with equal severity; he was immediately condemned by a court-martial, and executed on an eminence near one of his own castles, at Pontefract, in Yorkshire. The infatuated Monarch immediately recalled the Spencers, who now became more insolent and assuming than ever. The Queen and the whole kingdom were exasperated against them. This haughty and ambitious princess retired to the court of France, on a pretence of carrying the young Prince her son, to do homage for the Duchy of Guienne, which was held under that crown. She was followed by many of the discontented Barons, and declaring she would never return to England in peace, unless young Spencer was banished the kingdom, she levied an army to effect by force what she had little hopes to expect by entreaties. On her landing in England, she was joined by almost the whole kingdom.

The unfortunate Edward was obliged to seek for safety in flight; leaving his palace, he retired to Bristol, where he got on board a ship and attempted to steer for Ireland, but being driven by contrary winds on the coast of Wales, he was taken and brought prisoner to Kenilworth Castle.

The subsequent history of this unfortunate Monarch is truly dismal. He was deposed by Parliament, and his son, Edward the Third, declared King. From Kenilworth, he was removed to Berkeley Castle, where, after having been carried to Corfe Castle, and various parts of the kingdom, he was brought back again, and murdered in a most cruel way, at the instigation of the Queen, and her favourite, Mortimer.

In 1327, Henry, brother to the late Earl, was, by Edward the Third, restored to the Earldoms of Lancaster and Leicester, this Castle, and all his brother's estates. His son was afterwards, in the same reign, created Duke of Lancaster; but he dying without male issue, and leaving only two daughters, John of Gaunt, fourth son to King Edward the Third, married one of them, and obtained this Castle for her dower; and the King afterwards gave him the Dukedom of Lancaster.

He greatly enlarged the Castle, by adding various buildings to it; particularly the tower, with three stories of arches, at the north end of the hall, which still bears his name; and he very much encreased the strength of it, by adding turrets to the outer walls.

He died in 1399, and leaving issue, Henry,

surnamed Bolingbroke, (from the place of his birth,) who was afterwards Henry the Fourth, this Castle came a third time into the hands of the Crown, and continued so through several successive reigns.

Henry the Seventh united it to the Dukedom of Cornwall; and his son, Henry the Eighth, was at a considerable expence in repairing and ornamenting it. He removed the *Pleasons en Marais*, (apparently a building for little parties of pleasure,) from the low marshy grounds where it stood, to where the remains of it now are, within the walls near the Swan Tower.

It descended, after his death, regularly to his son Edward the Sixth, Queen Mary, and her sister Elizabeth; who, in 1563, granted it, with all the Royalties belonging to it, to Robert Dudley, third son to the Duke of Northumberland, who she soon afterwards created Earl of Leicester.

It was under this haughty favourite, that Kenilworth reached the summit of its grandeur. He, in 1571, erected the large pile of building on the south side of the inner court, which bears his name, and the great gate-house on the north; this he made the principal entrance, and changed the front of the Castle, which before was towards the lake. He likewise built a tower at each end of the tilt-yard, from whence the ladies had an opportunity of seeing the noble diversion of tilting and barriers; and greatly enlarged the lake, the chase, and the parks, which now extended over near twenty miles of country. He is said to have expended sixty thousand pounds, (an immense sum in those days,) in these magnificent improvements.

" HERE, in July, 1575, having completed
" all things for her reception, Lord Leicester
" entertained Queen Elizabeth for the space of
" seventeen days, with excessive cost, and a
" variety of delightful shews, as may be seen
" at large in a special discourse therefore then
" printed, and entitled *The Princely Pleasures*
" *of Kenilworth Castle.** At her first en-
" trance, there was a floating island upon the

---

* Written by Gascoigne, an attendant on the Court, and a Poet. It is printed in the last edition of his Poems.

" pool, bright blazing with torches; upon
" which, clad in silks, were the *Lady of the
" Lake,* and two nymphs waiting on her;
" who made a speech to the Queen in metre,
" of the antiquity and owners of the Castle;
" which was closed with cornets and loud
" music. Within the base-court there was a
" very goodly bridge set up, of twenty feet
" wide and seventy feet long, over which the
" Queen did pass. On each side thereof were
" posts erected, with presents upon them unto
" her, by the gods, viz.—A cage of wild fowls,
" by *Silvanus;* sundry rare fruits, by *Pomona;*
" of corn, by *Ceres;* of wine, by *Bacchus;*
" of sea-fish, by *Neptune;* of all the habili-
" ments of war, by *Mars;* and of musical
" instruments, by *Apollo.* And for the several
" days of her stay, various rare sports and
" shews were there exercised, viz.—In the
" chase, a savage man with satyrs; bear-bait-
" ings, fire-works, Italian tumblers, a country
" bridal, with running at the quintin,* and

---

* Running at the quintin, was a ludicrous kind of tilting, performed in the following manner:—A post, as high as a man on horseback, was set upright in the ground, with an iron pivot on the top, on which turned a long horizontal beam,

" morris-dancing. And, that there might be
" nothing wanting that these parts could afford,
" hither came the Coventry men, and acted
" the ancient play, long since used in that city,
" called *Hock's Tuesday*, setting forth the de-
" struction of the Danes, in King Etheldred's
" time; with which the Queen was so well
" pleased, that she gave them a brace of bucks,
" and five marks in money, to bear the charges
" of a feast.

---

unequally divided. To the upright post was fixed the figure of a man; the horizontal beam representing his arms; the shortest end had a target nearly covering the whole body, with a hole, in the shape of a heart, or ring, cut in the middle of it; and the longest was armed with a wooden sword, or a bag of sand. Peasants mounted on cart horses, run full tilt at this figure, and endeavoured to strike the heart with a pole made like a lance; if they succeeded, they were greatly applauded; but if they struck the shield instead of the heart, the short arm of the lever retiring, brought round the wooden sword or the sand bag with such velocity, as generally to unhorse the awkward assailant.—This amusement, somewhat diversified, was, not long ago, practised in Flanders, at their wakes and festivals. The revolving arms were placed vertically; the lower shewing the ring, while the upper one supported a vessel full of water, which emptying itself on the head of the unskilful tilter, punished his want of dexterity with a severe ducking.—*Beauties of British Antiquity*.

"Besides all this, he had, upon the pool, a *Triton*, riding on a Mermaid, eighteen feet long; as also, an *Arion* on a Dolphin, with rare music. And, to honour this entertainment the more, there were then knighted here, Sir Thomas Cecil, son and heir to the Lord Treasurer, Sir Henry Cobham, brother to Lord Cobham, Sir Francis Stanhope, and Sir Thomas Tresham.*

"The cost and expense of this entertainment may be guessed at, by the quantity of beer then drank, which amounted to three hundred and twenty hogsheads of the ordinary sort, as I have been credibly informed.

"Shortly after which, viz. the year next ensuing, Lord Leicester obtained, by grant of the said Queen, a weekly market here upon

---

* Rowland White has left us a curious account of the amusements of Elizabeth's reign, and with what spirit her Majesty pursued her pleasures, as late as her sixty-seventh year. "Her Majesty says she is very well. This day she appoints a Frenchman to do feats upon a rope in the Conduit Court. To-morrow, she hath commanded the Bears, the Bull, and the Ape to be bayted in the Tilt-yard. Upon Wednesday, she will have solemne dawncing."—*Pennant's London.*

"the Wednesday, and a fair yearly on Midsum-
"mer-day."

LORD Leicester left this Castle and estate by his will, to his brother, Ambrose, Earl of Warwick, for his life, and after his death, to Sir Robert Dudley, whom he did not then think proper to stile his lawful son.

THE Earl of Warwick dying, about a year afterwards, Sir Robert came into possession of them; and determined to prove his legitimacy, and assert his claim to his father's titles. The case was as follows:—Lord Leicester privately married the widow of Lord Sheffield, by whom he had this son; but, being apprehensive that the Queen would disapprove of his marriage, it was never made public. This the Earl afterwards basely took advantage of, and married Lady Essex, (whom he fell violently in love with,) though the Lady Sheffield was still living; and she (Lady Essex) had interest enough, after his death, to obtain a decree in the Star Chamber, by which all Sir Robert Dudley's proceedings, to prove his father's prior marriage with the Lady Sheffield, (which he had nearly accomplished,) were put a stop to; as a sentence in his favor must greatly have reflected on Lady Essex's character. Sir Robert now determined to leave a country, where he had met with such undeserved ill treatment, and soon after went abroad, and settled in Italy. His great learning and other rare endowments, raised him very high in the favor and esteem of the Grand Duke of Tuscany, and the Emperor Ferdinand the Second, who, in 1620, created him a Duke; whereupon he was generally called Duke of Northumberland, which title his grandfather bore till he forfeited it, by attainder, in the reign of Queen Mary. His (Sir Robert's) wife was the Duchess Dudley, (so created in the reign of Charles the First,) whose name is recorded in the church, as a considerable benefactress to this parish. His absence abroad, gave his enemies at home, an opportunity of raising a false clamour against him, and they procured a summons, under the privy seal, for his return; but he not complying with it, his Castle and estates were seized for the King's use, by the statute of fugitives. The following survey of them was then taken, which I have subjoined, as it shews the magnificence of the Castle at that time. It is copied from Dugdale:—

"The Castle of Kenilworth *situated on a rock*.

"1st. The circuit thereof, within the walls, containeth seven acres; upon which (the walls) the walks are so spacious and fair, that two or three persons together, may walk upon most places thereof.

"2nd. The Castle, with the four gatehouses, all built of free-stone, hewn and cut; the walls in many places ten and fifteen feet in thickness, some more, some less, the least four feet.

"3d. The Castle and four gatehouses, all covered with lead, whereby it is subject to no other decay but the glass, through the extremity of the weather.

"4th. The rooms of great state within the same; and such as are able to receive his Majesty, the Queen, and Prince, at one time; built with as much uniformity and conveniency as any houses of later times; and with such stately cellars, all carried upon pillars, and architecture of free-stone, carved and wrought, as the like are not within this kingdom; and also all other houses for offices answerable.

"5th. There lieth about the same, in chases and parks, twelve hundred pounds per annum; nine hundred whereof are grounds for pleasure, the rest in meadow and pasture thereunto adjoining, tenants and freeholders.

"6th. There joineth upon this ground, a park-like ground, called the King's Wood, with fifteen several coppices lying altogether, containing seven hundred and eighty-nine acres within the same; which, in the Earl of Leicester's time, were stored with red deer, since which the deer have strayed, but the ground is in no sort blemished, having great store of timber and other trees of much value upon the same.

"7th. There runneth through the same grounds, by the walls of the Castle, a *fair pool*, containing one hundred and eleven acres, well stored with fish and wild fowl: which, at pleasure, is to be let round the Castle.

"8th. In timber and woods upon the ground, to the value (as hath been offered) of twenty thousand pounds, (having a convenient time to remove them) which to his Majesty, in the survey, are valued at eleven thousand seven hundred and twenty-two pounds; which proportion, in a like measure, is held in all the rest upon the other values to his Majesty.

"9th. The circuit of the Castle, manors, parks, and chase, lying round together, contain, at least, nineteen or twenty miles, in a pleasant country; the like, both for strength, state, and pleasure, not being within the realm of England.

"10th. These lands have been surveyed by Commissioners from the King, and the Lord Privy Seal, with directions from his Lordship to find all things under their true worth, and upon the oath of jurors, as well freeholders as customary tenants; which course being held by them, are, notwithstanding, surveyed and returned at thirty-eight thousand five hundred and fifty-four pounds, fifteen shillings.

"Out of which, for Sir Robert Dudley's contempt, there is to be deducted, ten thousand pounds, and for the Lady Dudley's jointure, which is without impeachment of waste, whereby she may sell all the woods, which by the survey, amount to eleven thousand seven hundred and twenty-two pounds. The total of the survey ariseth as folloeth:—

	£.	s.	d.
In Land,	16,431	9	0
In Woods,	11,722	2	0
The Castle,	10,401	4	0
Total	£38,554	15	0*

"His Majesty hath herein the mean profits of the Castle and premises, through Sir Robert Dudley's contempt, during life, or his Majesty's pardon, the reversion in fee being in the Lord Privy Seal."

Prince Henry, (eldest son to James the First,) was very desirous of obtaining this Castle; which, as appears by the foregoing report, was one of the most magnificent places at that time in the kingdom. He made overtures to Sir Robert Dudley to purchase it, and offered him

---

* As the woods in this survey are valued at only £11,722. which had been offered £20,000. for, and the same proportion observed in the Castle and estates; the whole, therefore, instead of £38,554. as valued at in the estimate, must have been worth £65,780. and even this seems too small a sum, as Lord Leicester had so lately expended £60,000. here.

fourteen thousand five hundred pounds for his right in it; a sum greatly inadequate to its value; but Sir Robert foreseeing the little probability of his ever returning to England, accepted the offer, and the conveyances were accordingly executed. Three thousand pounds were to have been paid at the time; but, by the failure of the merchant who undertook to remit the money to Sir Robert, who was then in Italy, he did not receive it; and Prince Henry dying soon after, the remainder of the purchase-money was never paid. Nevertheless, Prince Charles took possession of it, as heir to his brother, and obtained a grant out of the Exchequer, for four thousand pounds to Sir Robert Dudley's wife, in lieu of her jointure. He kept it till he came to the crown; but, in the first year of his reign, he granted it to Robert Carey, Earl of Monmouth; Lord Carey, his eldest son; and Thomas Carey, Esq. It continued in their hands during the reign of King Charles; but after his death, Oliver Cromwell gave the whole manor to several of his officers, who stripped, and partly demolished the Castle; drained the lake, cut down the woods, and destroyed the parks and chase; they divided the land into farms, which they continued to hold, till the Restoration again altered the face of things. King Charles the Second renewed the lease, granted by his father, to the Earl of Monmouth's daughters; but it being again almost expired, he granted the reversion of the whole manor, to Lawrence Lord Hyde, (second son to Lord Chancellor Clarendon,) whom he created Baron of Kenilworth Castle, and Earl of Rochester. His Lordship died in 1711, and was succeeded in his titles and estate by Henry, his only son; who, in 1723, by the death of Edward, third Earl of Clarendon, succeeded likewise to that Earldom. But he dying in 1753, and leaving no male issue, his granddaughter, Lady Charlotte Capel, (by William Capel, Earl of Essex, and the Lady Jane Hyde, his wife,) became (her mother being before dead) the representative of the Hyde family; and, pursuant to the will of the said Henry Earl of Clarendon and Rochester, she took the name and arms of Hyde. Her Ladyship, in 1752, was married to the Honourable Thomas Villers, second son to the Earl of Jersey; who was, by King George the Second, in 1756, created Lord Hyde, of Hindon, in the County of Wilts, and had the further honour of the Earldom of Clarendon conferred upon him by his present

Majesty, in 1776. His Lordship died the 15th of December, 1786, leaving this Castle, and his estates in Warwickshire, to his eldest son, the present Earl of Clarendon.

Having now traced out the history of the Castle, from its foundation to the present time, nothing further remains, but to give a description of its present state. I mean not to paint the magnificence or beauty of its ruins, (that would indeed be a much properer subject for the pencil than the pen,) but merely to give strangers a clue, that may enable them to walk over the remains of this noble pile with greater satisfaction, from knowing the different parts as they go along. In this they will be greatly assisted by the plan of the Castle, which I have annexed, principally for that purpose.

You enter from the north, by the side of the great gate-house, built by Lord Leicester; the wall and ditch formerly joined it, and you entered the Castle under an arched way, between the four turrets; but, on its being made an habitation, it was walled up, and formed into two large rooms. One of them is fitted up with an elegant chimney-piece and an oak wainscot, taken from Leicester-buildings, and is worthy attention.

I would advise every stranger to see it; an indulgence they will readily obtain, from the civility of the people who live in the house. The large pile of building on the right hand, (absurdly called *Cæsar's Tower,*) is the strongest and most ancient part of the Castle, and served as a kind of fortress to it in times of danger; three sides of the wall are entire, the fourth side was pulled down by Oliver Cromwell's soldiers, in order to make use of the materials. It seemingly consisted of one vast room on a floor, and a variety of closets formed in the walls, which in some places are sixteen feet thick. The great staircase was in the south-west angle of the building. Some of the paintings on the walls are still visible. The three kitchens lie beyond it, and reached nearly from *Cæsar's Tower* to Lancaster-buildings; they were very large; some traces of foundations on the greensward, is all that now remains of them, and only serves to shew their situation. Lancaster-buildings come next, they were very strong; the three ranges of arches one above another, are still to be seen. You should climb over them to the top of the wall, (which the ruined state of the building, and the rubbish that has fallen down, render no difficult task,) from whence you have a very fine view of the country, with the house and church at Honiley, in the back-ground. One cannot stand here a moment, without being struck with the idea of what a glorious prospect this must have been, with the vallies on either hand, filled with the transparent waters of the lake, surrounded with a beautiful variety of pleasure-ground, laid out in lawns and woods. In coming down again, you have the great hall on your right hand; a noble room, eighty-six feet long, and forty-five feet wide, well adapted to the hospitable days of our forefathers. Underneath the hall, was a room of the same dimensions, for the domestics, and those numerous guests who were not entitled to a place at the upper table. Towards the south end of the hall, on the east side, there is a large bow window, and opposite to it, a recess, that probably served as a kind of sideboard, beyond which there is a small closet, which the common people have ridiculously named, *Queen Elizabeth's Dressing-room*. You now come to the range of apartments that formed the south side of the inner court, consisting of the White-hall, the Presence-chamber, and the Privy-chamber, of which there is nothing remaining but the fragments of walls and staircases, and a part of two large bow windows: the inner one is, like those of the hall, hung with ivy in a very picturesque way. Indeed, the ivy, that covers these ruins, forms one of the greatest ornaments. Leicester-buildings, though the last erected, seem likely to be the first part that will totally fall to decay. Time has already made great havoc with this noble pile, and some part or other annually moulders away under his ruthless hand. But still far greater have been the depredations caused by avarice. Vast quantities of materials have been fetched from hence, for the various purposes of building, repairing roads, &c. and it is to the benevolent attention of the late Earl of Clarendon, that we owe what now remains. His Lordship was careful to preserve the ruins from destruction, and prevented the loose materials from being applied to such improper uses. Proceeding round Leicester-buildings to the right, you come to the west front, which is more uniform than any of the Castle. The light arch fronting you, leads through what was formerly called *Plaisance*,

CPSIA information can be obtained
at www.ICGtesting.com
Printed in the USA
BVHW051343161120
593415BV00014B/895